Bardaisan and His Disciples

Analecta Gorgiana

158

Series Editor
George Kiraz

Analecta Gorgiana is a collection of long essays and short monographs which are consistently cited by modern scholars but previously difficult to find because of their original appearance in obscure publications. Carefully selected by a team of scholars based on their relevance to modern scholarship, these essays can now be fully utilized by scholars and proudly owned by libraries.

Bardaisan and His Disciples

Early Eastern Christianity

F. C. Burkitt

gorgias press

2009

Gorgias Press LLC, 180 Centennial Ave., Piscataway, NJ, 08854, USA

www.gorgiaspress.com

Copyright © 2009 by Gorgias Press LLC

Originally published in 1904

All rights reserved under International and Pan-American Copyright Conventions. No part of this publication may be reproduced, stored in a retrieval system or transmitted in any form or by any means, electronic, mechanical, photocopying, recording, scanning or otherwise without the prior written permission of Gorgias Press LLC.

2009

ISBN 978-1-60724-130-0

ISSN 1935-6854

This volume is an extract of the Gorgias Press edition of *Early Eastern Christianity: St. Margaret's Lectures 1904 on the Syriac-Speaking Church*, originally published by John Murray, 1904.

Printed in the United States of America

LECTURE V

BARDAISAN AND HIS DISCIPLES

As Renan said long ago, and as William Wright repeats in the opening words of his Short History of Syriac Literature, the characteristic of the Syrians is a certain mediocrity. They shone neither in war, nor in the arts, nor in science. They lacked the poetic fire of the older Hebrews and of the Arabs. But they were apt enough as pupils of the Greeks; they assimilated and reproduced, adding little or nothing of their own. There was no *Alfarabi*, no *Avicenna*, no *Averroës*, in the cloisters of Edessa, Qinnesrîn, or Nisibis. The Syrian Church of the fourth and succeeding centuries failed to produce men who rose to the level of a Eusebius, a Gregory Nazianzen, a Basil, and a Chrysostom. "The literature of Syria," says Dr Wright, "is, on the whole, not an attractive one." I am not going to challenge this severe verdict on the general ground. Syriac Literature presents the depressing spectacle of a steady Decline and

Fall, following the general collapse of civilisation in the East. Moreover what we have of it is a specialised department. The Syriac Literature that has come down to us is not, like the literature of the Greeks or Arabs, a selection of almost all the departments of human activity. What we have in Syriac is practically nothing more than the contents of a very fine monastic Library. Many departments of profane literature are but little represented and even the ancient heretics are rarely allowed to speak to us, except through the imperfect medium of orthodox refutations.

What we have of Syriac Literature is, taken in the lump, dull. But there are some indications that outside the walls of the orthodox cloisters there was in early times some independent life and light, and a little has percolated through to us. I propose in the present Lecture to illustrate this side of Syriac Literature from the one philosophical work of the School of Bardaisan that has come down to us.

Bardaisan, called "The last of the Gnostics," a man distinguished by birth, by learning, by intelligence, became a Christian during the last quarter of the second century. He died in the year 222 A.D., having by that time separated himself from the organisation of the Church of his native place. Later ages regarded him as a heretic; and when the sect that had been formed by his followers died out, the monastic libraries did not greatly care to preserve even the orthodox confutations of his doctrine. We are therefore obliged to reconstruct from scattered notices and the ill-informed partisan statements of later chroniclers our picture of the only original thinker which the Syriac Church helped to mould.

Let us first hear what Eusebius has to tell us, writing barely a century after the death of Bardaisan. Eusebius (*HE* iv 30) says that Bardesanes (as the Greeks called *Bardaiṣân*) was a most competent writer in his native Syriac, and that he wrote treatises against Marcion and other heretics, some of which had been translated into Greek. Among these was a Dialogue on Fate addressed to "Antoninus," by whom Eusebius (or his source) may have meant Caracalla, or even Elagabalus. We are told further that Bardesanes had been a disciple of Valentinus the Gnostic, but that he abandoned his teaching for more orthodox views, yet without ever quite shaking off the old slough of heretical opinion. Eusebius gives no exact dates, but puts Bardaisan under Pope Soter, *i.e.* about 179, the traditional date of his conversion to Christianity.

BARDAISAN AND HIS DISCIPLES

Epiphanius tells us more, but as usual it is not safe to trust all that this amiable Father of the Church says about a heretic. He evidently regarded the accession of Bardaisan to Christianity as one of the results of the conversion of the blessed King Abgar. He seems however to have some knowledge of Bardaisan's works, for he tells us quite truly that the Dialogue on Fate was written against the doctrines of a certain 'Awîda the Astrologer.[1] But whereas Eusebius tells us that Bardaisan had been a follower of Valentinus and never quite shook off his heresy, Epiphanius makes him become a follower of Valentinus after he had been orthodox.

The fullest account of Bardaisan is that inserted in the Syriac Chronicle of Michael the Great, Jacobite Patriarch of Antioch from 1166 to 1199. We have already had occasion to discuss this account in the first of these Lectures when considering the early episcopal succession to the See of Edessa, but it may not be out of place to remind you once again how circumspect we ought to be in trusting to details preserved in so late a source. Bardaisan lived a thousand years before the Patriarch Michael compiled his Chronicle, and we can only regard the Chronicle

---

[1] Αὐειδὰν τὸν ἀστρονόμον (*Oehler* i, pt. 2, p. 144, note).

as a serious source of historical information in those passages where there is good reason to believe that Michael and his predecessors have all copied faithfully from a much older source. In the present case we have to allow for ignorance and prejudice: ignorance, because the learning and the philosophy of an independent thinker are not easily packed into the compendiums of annalists, and prejudice, because Bardaisan's name was chiefly known in later ages as that of a great heretic and schismatic, and it was assumed that he must have been immoral and irrational. With these reservations let us take Michael's account.

After declaring how Bardaisan was converted in 179 A.D. by Bishop Hystasp of Edessa, and ordained by him a Deacon (!)[1] Michael mentions that Bardaisan wrote treatises against heresies and that he turned to the doctrines of Valentinus. He then goes on to tell us: "Bardaisan says that there are three chief Natures (*K'yânê*) and four existences (*Îthyê*), which are Reason and Power and Understanding and Knowledge. The four Powers are Fire and Water and Light and Spirit (or Wind), and from these come the other existences of the world[2] to the number

---

[1] Chabot, *Michel le Syrien* [110].
[2] The MS. has "and the world."

of 360. And Bardaisan says that He who spake with Moses and the Prophets was the Chief of the Angels and not God Himself; our Lord was clothed with the body of an Angel and [from][1] Mary the shining Soul was clothed which thus took form and body. Furthermore the Upper Powers gave man his soul and the Lower Powers gave him his limbs: the Sun gave the brain, and the Moon and the Planets gave the other parts." Then follow some almost unintelligible remarks about the syzygy of the Sun and Moon, whereby the material world is renewed every month. Michael then informs us that according to Bardaisan "the Messiah, the Son of God, was born under the planet Jupiter, crucified in the hour of Mars, buried in the hour of Mercury, and in the time of Jupiter He arose from the grave." Bardaisan also said that the dead do not rise and that dreams are true, and marriage he calls a good purification.[2] He had three sons, Abgarôn, Hasdu, and Harmonius, who all remained true to his doctrines.

It is difficult to extract from this confused farrago of statements anything certain about

---

[1] The MS. omits "from."
[2] So Bar Hebraeus understands the passage from which Michael quotes.

THE DIALOGUE ON FATE 161

the real nature of Bardaisan's teaching. At the same time some of the statements above quoted are confirmed from other sources, such as the express declaration in Ephraim's Treatise against False Doctrines (*Ad Hypatium*, bk. ii, in *Overbeck*, p. 63) that Bardaisan had said that the human Soul was mixed and compounded of seven constituents. Unfortunately the latter part of this valuable prose Treatise exists only as an almost illegible palimpsest which still awaits a decipherer.[1] The metrical discourses of Ephraim against Heretics must also be used with great caution, for the very reason that they are written in metre. It is difficult to quote one's adversary accurately, if you are tied down to a verse of five syllables to the line.

Fortunately we are not entirely obliged to gain our knowledge of Bardaisan from refutations of his opinions. The *Dialogue on Fate*, mentioned by Eusebius and Epiphanius, has been actually preserved. Like so many other treasures of Syriac literature it was discovered

---

[1] What Overbeck has published is only the First Book and about half the Second There were originally Five Books, each beginning in turn with the five letters of Ephraim's name (A F R Y M). The palimpsest mentioned in the text is B.M. Add. 14623.

L

by Dr Cureton, when Keeper of the Oriental MSS. at the British Museum and also Rector of this Church of S. Margaret's, Westminster.

A surprise meets us at the outset. This famous Dialogue, mentioned by several Fathers in a Greek translation, and actually in large part incorporated into more than one ancient Christian writing, does not profess to be the work of Bardaisan, but of his disciple Philip. Bardaisan himself is the chief speaker and teaches with authority, but Philip writes in the first person. This Philip is otherwise entirely unknown, and the name, so common in Greek, is rarely met with among the Syrians. Thus the suspicion arises whether he is anything more than a literary device. In any case there is no reason to suppose that there is any analogy between the parts played by Bardaisan and Philip in the *De Fato* with those of Socrates and Plato in the Platonic Dialogues. A truer literary analogy would be found between S. Paul and that Tertius who wrote the Epistle to the Romans.

A further formal difficulty is to be found in the name of the Dialogue. The Greek writers who know of it speak of it as a treatise *On Fate*, a very suitable description. But the Syriac MS. is headed, "The Book of the Laws of Countries," and some modern writers have assumed that this is the true title. I incline however to believe that the Greeks were right, and that the Syriac heading of our MS. is not so much the original title as an indication of the cause of its preservation. It is inconceivable that a work of the heresiarch Bardaisan or of his immediate disciples should have been intentionally preserved except on a side issue. A side issue is actually provided by the interesting descriptions of heathen customs and laws mentioned at the end of the Dialogue. The customs are curious reading in themselves and they are mentioned in illustration of the disciplinary power of Christianity. For the sake of the mention of these customs the Dialogue was valued in later times, and from the description of them it acquired this name of the " Book of the Laws of Countries." But the work as a whole is really about Fate, and it is more appropriate to continue to call it the Dialogue *On Fate*.

The Dialogue opens with narrative: whoever " Philip " may have been, he was certainly master of a pleasant style and the art of arranging his material. " A few days ago," he says, " we went in to pay a call on our brother Shamshagram, and there Bardaisan came and found us ; and when he had inquired and found him well, he asked us what we were talking about, 'for,' said he, 'I heard the sound of your conversation outside when I was coming in.' For it was his custom, whenever he found us talking, to ask us what it was about, that he might speak thereon with us. And we said to him: 'Awida here was saying to us, "If God is one, as you say, and He constituted the race of men, and really wills what you are commanded to do, why did He not constitute them so that they could not go wrong, but always do what is good? For in that case His will would be done."'"

The problem is not exactly a new one, but even after many centuries the solution is not in our hands. Let us see how this school of Christian Philosophers looked at the question.

Bardaisan first replies: "Tell me, my son Awida, do you mean that there is not One who is God over all, or do you mean that the One God does not intend that men should conduct themselves justly and rightly?" Awida answers that he asked his friends to see what they would say first, as he was shy of asking Bardaisan himself. Bardaisan assures him that those who come with a sincere desire to learn the truth and to set forth genuinely felt difficulties have no reason to be shy; it is the duty of the Master to attempt to answer such difficulties when

WHY THE ONE GOD ALLOWS ERROR 165

they are put forth. Awida then says that his difficulties are genuinely his own, but that Bardaisan's disciples would not persuade him by arguments and kept saying, "you have only to believe and you will be able to know everything," and Awida on the other hand said that he could not believe, except he was shown reason for doing so.

Here we approach the real teaching of the Dialogue. Bardaisan does not reply directly to Awida, but turns to his own disciples, saying: "It is not Awida alone who does not wish to believe. Many others are in the same case, and because there is no faith in them they cannot be shown reason, but they are continually pulling down and building up, and the end is a mere shapeless ruin in which knowledge of truth cannot dwell. But (he continues) since Awida says he does not wish to believe, I will talk to you that do believe about the question which he has asked, and thus he may hear something more." So Bardaisan begins to say: "Many men there are who from lack of faith have difficulty even in listening to instruction, because they have no foundation to build on and are even in doubt about God Himself. Such men have not that Fear of God which delivers us from all fears, but are at the same time timid and rash. Now as to the question that Awida asks, why God has not made us so that we could not sin and so not be guilty before Him, I reply that if man had been so made he would not be himself, but a machine. Man would be like a harp on which the performer plays: the praise and the blame, and even the very knowledge of how the instrument is being used, belong to the musician and not to the harp. But God in His kindness did not wish to make man thus, and so He endowed men with much greater freedom than many things, equal in fact with the angels. For look (said he) at the Sun and the Moon and the Planets, and all the rest of those things which are so much greater than we in some respects: to these freedom in themselves has not been given, but they are all so fixed that they can only move in the path marked out for them. The Sun cannot say, 'I will not appear at the right time,' the Moon cannot say, 'I will not wax and wane,' the Stars must rise and set when they are due, the Sea cannot help carrying the ships, the Mountains and the Earth cannot help remaining each in its place; for all these things are mere vehicles of the Wisdom of God that never goes wrong. If everything was only formed to be useful for something else, for whose benefit would the world be made? And if everything was only formed to receive benefits, how would the service of the world be supplied? As it is, no things are wholly detached one from the other; for an absolutely self-contained power or thing would be an Element which has not yet received its place in the organisation of the universe. The things needed for human use have been placed within the sphere of human activity. This is what is meant when we read in Genesis that man was made in the image of God. Out of the Divine Kindness it was given to man that the things needful for his life should be his servants during this present dispensation, and that he should conduct himself as he pleases. What is in his power to do, he can do if he pleases, and can leave undone if he pleases. He can, in a word, control himself or fail to control himself, and the praise or blame which his conduct deserves is really his own. See then (continues Bardaisan) how greatly the goodness of God has been exercised towards men, in that so much more freedom has been given to man than to other things, that by means of it he may control himself, and so act the part of God and be reckoned with the Angels. For Angels also have freedom such as men have, as we may see from the story in Genesis of those Sons of God who mingled themselves with the daughters of men. Had they not done this they would not have fallen from their exalted station and received their due need of punishment; and similarly we may infer that those which did not fall thus, but kept control of themselves when exposed to temptation, were exalted and hallowed and became the recipients of great gifts. For every being that exists has need of the Lord of all, and to His gifts there is no end; yet know this (says Bardaisan), that even those things which are governed by fixed laws, as I said, are nevertheless not entirely deprived of all freedom, and therefore at the last all of them are subject to Judgment."

Then I said: "And how are those things judged whose movements are fixed beforehand?"

He saith to me: "The powers of Nature, O Philip, are not judged in respect of what they have been *made* to do, but in respect of what they have been *entrusted* to do. For the Elements are not deprived of their nature when they are assigned their place in the Universe, but the vehemence of their peculiar properties is lessened by the mixture of one with the other, and moreover they are under subjection to the power of Him who made them. Yet in so far as they are in subjection they are not brought to judgment, but only in respect of what is in their own power."

After this Awida says to Bardaisan: "All this that you have said is excellent, but how strict are the commandments that have been given to men! They cannot be performed."

Bardaisan replied: "This is the utterance of one who does not really wish to do what is good, one who obeys the Enemy of man and is subject to him. For nothing has been commanded to men but what they are able to do. There are two commandments set before us, very fit and proper exercises for our free nature: the one is, that we should abstain from everything that is evil and that we hate to be done to us, and the other, that we should do what is good and what we like to be done to us. For what man is physically unable to keep from stealing or lying or adultery or malicious false witness? All these things belong to the mind of man, to his disposition, not to his material lot. Even if a man be poor or diseased or old or crippled he can abstain from doing these evil deeds; and just as he can abstain from these things, so also he can love and bless and speak truth and pray for the welfare of everyone he knows. And if he be well and have the opportunity of giving something of his own, he can do so; he can use the material force at his command for the support of the weak. There is no one who cannot do this. In fact, the Commandments of God are concerned with those very matters which are within the range of human control. We are not commanded to carry heavy burdens of stone or wood or anything else, which only those who are strong of body are able to do;[1] nor to build towns and found cities, which only kings are able to do; nor to steer ships, which only sailors have skill to manage; nor to survey land and divide it, which only surveyors know how to do; nor to practise any other of the arts, which some can do and the rest are shut out from. To us through God's kindness such equable commandments have been given as every living man can do with pleasure; for there is no one who does not rejoice when he is doing well, and no one who keeps himself from doing hateful deeds who

---

[1] The same argument is curiously repeated in the Acts of Thomas (*Wright* 253; E. Trans., p. 219): "For we are not commanded to do anything which we are unable to do, nor to take up heavy burdens, nor to build buildings, which carpenters build for themselves with wisdom, nor to practise the art of hewing stones, which stone-cutters know as their craft; but we are commanded to do something which we can do,—to refrain from fornication, the head of all evils, and from murder, etc." The ethical theory is the same, and I venture to suggest that both 'Philip' and the author of the *Acts of Thomas* derived it from Bardaisan. The question is important to us from its bearing on the authorship of the *Hymn of the Soul*. See p. 199.

does not feel at ease in himself—except indeed those who have not been created for good and who are called Tares. For the Judge of all is not so unjust as to blame man for what he cannot do."

Awida then said: "Do you say of these things, O Bardaisan, that they are easy to do?"

Bardaisan replies: "To him that *wishes* to do them I said, and still say, that they are easy, for they are the appropriate course for the mind of a free man to take and for a soul that has not rebelled against those who control it. But in bodily activities many things interfere with the ideal course, especially old age and sickness and poverty."

Awida says: "Perhaps one may keep from doing wrong, but who among men is able to do good?"

This Bardaisan denies, declaring that doing good is the natural action of man, while doing evil is really unnatural and the work of the Enemy; evil, in fact, is a disease. To do good gives real pleasure; the pleasure we may get from evil is as different from this as the quiet that comes from exhaustion and despair differs from the quiet we get in health. Desire is one thing, Love is another; Christian charity is not mere good-fellowship. "The counterfeit of Love is Desire. Desire may have satisfaction for an hour, but it is far from being true Love, whose satisfaction has neither corruption nor dissolution for ever."

The writer of the Dialogue then remarks: "Awida was saying that men do wrong from their nature: if men had not been designed to do wrong, they would not do wrong."

Bardaisan says: "If all men acted the same way, and had only one set of opinions, we should conclude that their actions were the result of their nature, and that they had no freedom such as I have been describing to you. But that you may understand what is Nature and what is Freedom, I shall go on to point out to you that the Nature of man is to be born, to grow up, to arrive at full age, to beget and to grow old, eating and drinking, sleeping and waking, and finally to die. These things, because they are part of the Nature of man, belong to all men; and not to men only, but also to everything that has life, in fact, some of them are shared even by plants. This belongs to the sphere of the physical constitution of everything, whereby it is made, created, and set in the world, each according to its own laws. Furthermore we find the laws of Nature are uniformly observed by the various animals. The lion eats meat by Nature, and therefore all lions are eaters of meat; the sheep eats grass by Nature, and therefore all sheep are eaters of grass. All bees, all ants, store up food for themselves in the same way; all scorpions are ready to sting without being attacked. All the animals keep their own laws: the eaters of flesh do not become eaters of grass, nor do the eaters of grass become eaters of flesh.

"But men do not behave in this way. In the affairs of their bodies they keep the laws of their nature like beasts, but in the affairs of their minds they do what they will, acting as if they were free or at least entrusted with freedom, after the image of God. For some of them eat meat and no bread, some of them distinguish between various sorts of foods, and some of them eat nothing that has had in it the breath of life. There are some who have intercourse with their mothers, their sisters, and their daughters; others keep altogether from women. There are some who are fierce as lions and leopards; and some who hurt those who have done them no wrong, like the scorpion; and some that are driven like sheep and do no harm to those that drag them along. Some act with kindness, some with justice, some with malice; and if any one say that he is only acting in accordance with his Nature, a little reflection will show that this is not the case. For there are some who used to be adulterers and drunkards, but when a discipline of good counsel reached them they have become modest and temperate, and have despised the desire of their bodies; and there are some who used to live modestly and temperately, but when they neglected right discipline, they have resisted the commands of God and of their teachers, have fallen from the way of truth and have become adulterers and prodigals. And some have repented again, and have returned in fear to the truth in which they stood. Which, then, is the Nature of man? For lo, they are all different one from the other in their way of life and in their desires, and they that hold in a certain opinion and way of thinking resemble each other in their ways. Nevertheless, men who as yet are subject to the enticements of their desires and are led by their passions wish to lay the faults they commit at the door of their Maker, so that they may be considered faultless themselves. The moral law does not apply to that which belongs to Nature: no one is to be blamed for being tall or short, or white or black, or for any bodily defect, but a man deserves blame for thieving or lying or cursing and such like. Whence it may be seen that for the things which are not in our power, but come to us from Nature, we are not held guilty, nor can we control them; but for the things that belong to our freedom, if we do well the verdict is for us and we are deserving of praise, while if we do evil we are guilty and deserve blame."

At this point of the Dialogue comes in the famous disquisition on Fate. "We asked him," says Philip, "whether there are not some who say that men are controlled by the decrees of Fate, sometimes in an evil direction, sometimes in a good direction."

Bardaisan replies: "I well know, O Philip, that some of those men who are called Chaldæans, and others also, have a love for this very knowledge of the Art, as I also once had myself, for it has been said by me elsewhere that the mind of man yearns to know what most folk do not know, and this these persons think they do, holding that all the faults they commit and all the good they do and all that befalls them in wealth and in poverty, in sickness and in health and in bodily injury, come to them from the action of the so-called Seven Stars or Planets, and are controlled by their motions. There are others who say in opposition to these either that this Art is all a lie of the Chaldæans or that there is no such thing as Fate, and that all things both great and small are really in men's own power, and that diseases and bodily defects are mere matters of chance. Others again say that everything a man does he does of his own will through the Freedom given to him, and that defects and diseases and other misfortunes which befall are a punishment from God. Now in my humble opinion (says Bardaisan), it seems to me that these three opinions have each of them something that is true and something that is false. They are true, inasmuch as men speak according to what they actually see around them, and we cannot help noticing how things turn out adversely against us; but they are false, inasmuch as the Wisdom of God is richer than they, that Wisdom which established the worlds and created man and appointed the rulers of the various powers of the Universe, and gave to all things a responsibility suitable to each one of them. For I say that the authority possessed by the various orders of the Universe of which I have spoken —Gods,[1] Angels, Authorities, Celestial Rulers, Elements, Men, and Beasts—the authority given to each and all of them is partial. There is only One who has universal authority. But the others have authority in some matters and not in others, as I have already said; that in so far as they have authority the kindness of God may appear,

---

[1] Evidently we should read *lalâhê*, in the plural.

and in so far as they have no authority they may know that they have a supreme Lord.

"There is therefore such a thing as Fate, as the Chaldæans say. But that not everything happens according to our will is obvious from this, that most men desire to be rich and powerful and healthy and successful, and as a matter of fact only a few are so, and that not completely nor during all their life. Some have children and cannot rear them, some rear them only to prove a disgrace and a sorrow. Moreover men are not equally fortunate in all things; one man is rich as he likes to be, but unhealthy as he does not like to be, and another is healthy as he likes to be, but poor as he does not like to be. Some have many things they want and a few things they do not want, and some have a few things they want and many things they do not want. And thus we see that wealth and honours and health and sickness and children, and the various objects of desire are placed under Fate and not under our authority; but in the case of such of these things as happen according to our wish we accept them willingly and are pleased, and when they happen against our wish we are compelled to accept them whether we like or no. From the things which happen to us against our wish we see how it really stands with what we do wish: it is not because we will them that we get them, but they happen as they happen, and with some of the things we are pleased and with some of them not. And so we men are found to be governed by Nature equally, by Fate diversely, and by our Freedom as each man likes.

"But now we will go on to show that Fate and its dominion does not extend over everything. What we call 'Fate' is really the arrangement of the course marked out to the heavenly Powers and to the Elements by God. According to this arrangement the various faculties are assorted as they come down into the soul and the various souls are assorted as they come down into the bodies, and the agency by which this sorting is done is called the Fate and the Nativity of the congeries out of which the individual is evolved, all to help on that design which God in His mercy and grace has deigned to help and continues to do so until the consummation of all things.

"The body therefore is governed by Nature, and the soul suffers and perceives with it, and Fate cannot help or hinder the body against its Nature. Fate cannot give a man or woman children at a time when they are too young or too old by Nature to have children. Nor can Fate keep a man's body alive without eating and drinking, nor even when a man has food and drink can Fate keep a man so that he shall not die, for these and many other things belong to Nature. But when the conditions of Nature are complied with, within this limited field Fate comes into play, and it makes things to differ one with the other, sometimes helping and sometimes hindering the ordinary operation of Nature. Thus from Nature comes the growth of the body and its arrival at maturity, but apart from Nature and by Fate come sicknesses and defects in the body. From Nature comes the natural inclination of man and woman, but from Fate comes repugnance and also unnatural lusts. From Nature comes birth and children, but from Fate comes miscarriage and other failures. From Nature there is sufficiency in moderation for all, but from Fate comes on the one hand need and distress for food, and on the other extravagance and unnecessary luxury. Nature requires that elders should be the judges of youths, and wise men of fools, and that the strong should rule the weak and brave men command cowards; but Fate makes children to be the chiefs of elders and fools the chiefs of wise men, and that in time of war weak men command the strong and cowards command the brave. Know this especially (continued Bardaisan), that whenever the course of Nature is disturbed, the disturbance comes from this that I call Fate; and the reason of it is that the various Powers over which Fate is set are contrary one to the other, and some of them —those which we say are on the *right* hand —help Nature and add to its beauty, when the course of things is in their favour and they are in the ascendant in the heavenly Sphere, in their own portions; while others—which we say are on the *left*—are malignant, and when they are in the ascendant they are opposed to Nature, and they injure not men only, but beasts and plants and crops from time to time, as well as the seasons and fountains of water, everything, in fact, that is in Nature which is under their control. And it is because of these divisions and contrarieties between the Powers that some men have supposed that the world is governed without Providence, because they do not know that this contrariety and division of the Powers and their consequent conquest and defeat are the result of the free constitution that was given them from God, that these created things also by their own delegated powers might either conquer or be defeated.

"As we have seen that Fate destroys the work of Nature, so may we see the Freedom of man repelling Fate and destroying its work; yet not in everything, just as Fate cannot in everything repel Nature. For these three things, Nature, Fate and Freedom, must be kept in being, until the appointed course be fulfilled and the measure and the number of the days be accomplished, and all Beings and Natures have had their full existence."

Here Bardaisan stops for a moment, having come to a pause in his description of the forces by which all individuals are swayed. According to him, Nature determines the general conditions of each individual's existence, Fate determines the career, while the Freedom (or, as we say, the Free-will) of the individual is chiefly active in determining his character.

Awida now begins to be persuaded. He confesses himself satisfied that it is not from Nature that a man does wrong, and he sees that all men are not equally subjected to the same influences. Now he asks if it can be proved that it is not from Fate that men do wrong. "If this can be shown," he says, "we must believe that a man really possesses Freedom, and that by Nature he is brought to what is good and warned against what is bad;

and so he is justly liable to judgment at the last day."

Bardaisan replies: "From the fact that all men are not equally subjected to the same influences you are persuaded that it is not from their common Nature that men do wrong. Well then, you will be obliged to agree that it is not entirely from their Fate that they act wrongly if we can show you that the decree of the Fates and Powers do not equally affect all men, but that we really have some Freedom in ourselves not to serve physical Nature and not to be moved by the control of the heavenly Powers."

Awida says: "Show me this and I will believe and do whatever you tell me."

The reply of Bardaisan was in ancient times the most famous part of the whole Dialogue, and in a Greek dress it was borrowed wholesale by Eusebius and by the author of the *Clementine Recognitions*. But we need not linger very long over its curious erudition, except so far as concerns his descriptions of the "new race" of Christians. Speaking as an astrologer to an astrologer, Bardaisan reminds Awida that according to the rules of the Art each individual's Fate follows from the configuration of the heavenly bodies at the time of birth. But he runs through the nations of the earth

THE VARIED CUSTOMS OF NATIONS 183

from the Chinese on the east to the Britons on the west. Each nation has its own customs of marriage, of social life, of morals. But the inhabitants of these various countries are not all born at the same time, at the same configuration of the heavens. It is therefore not their Fate that compels the several nations each to keep their own customs and to avoid those of other people. For instance, says Bardaisan, in the whole of Media all men when they die, even while life is still remaining in them, are cast to the dogs and the dogs eat the dead of the whole of Media;[1] but we cannot say that all the Medians are born when the Moon is in conjunction with Mars in the constellation Cancer during the day below the Earth, as ought to be the case by the rules of Astrology for those who are to be eaten by dogs. The varied customs of the people of the earth prove that Fate does not act in the mechanical way that the Astrologers believe: the customs of the various countries, whether indigenous or forced upon the inhabitants by foreign rulers, are the result of human Free-will and are not

---

[1] See *Strabo* xi 517, quoted by E. R. Bevan, *House of Seleucus* i 290. The reason of the custom was of course to prevent the sacred elements of Earth, Air, Fire, and Water, from being polluted by a dead body.

due to the operations of Fate. It was not Fate, but the decree of King Abgar when he was converted to Christianity, that stopped the people of Edessa from mutilating themselves in honour of Atargatis. And so Bardaisan comes at last to his own Church.

"What then," he says, "shall we say of the new race of us Christians, whom in every country and in every region the Messiah established at His coming? For lo, all of us wherever we be are called Christians by the one Name of the Messiah; and on one day, the first of the week, we assemble together, and on specified days we abstain from food. And of these national customs, our brethren abstain from all that are contrary to their profession. Parthian Christians do not take two wives, Jewish Christians are not circumcised. Our sisters among the Bactrians do not practise promiscuity with strangers. Our Persian brethren do not take their daughters to wife; our Median brethren do not desert their dying relatives or bury them alive or throw them to the dogs. Nor do Christians in Edessa kill their wives or sisters that commit fornication, as the heathen Edessenes do, but they keep apart from them and commit them to the judgment of God. Nor do Christians in

Hatra stone thieves. But in whatever place they are, neither do the national laws separate them from the Law of the Messiah, nor does the Fate arranged by the Powers compel them to make use of what is impure to them. Yet sickness and health, and riches and poverty, matters that are not within their Free-will, these befall them wherever they are. For as the Free-will of men is not regularly governed by the compulsion of the Seven Planets, and even when so governed is able to withstand them, so also it remains true that man as we see him cannot easily get free from the orders of his governing influences, for he is a slave and put in subjection.

"To sum up, if we were really free to do everything, we should be everything; and if we were wholly without power to act, we should be mere machines in the hand of others. But when God so wills, everything can happen without disturbance, for His great and holy Will nothing can hinder. Those who think they can resist are in a position not of strength, but of evil and of error, and such a position may stand for a short time, because He is kind and permits all Natures to stand where they do and to be governed by their own will, yet bound by what has been done and by the constitution of things that was made for their help. For by the order and governance that has been given to things and the mixture of one principle with another the vehemence of the various Natures is weakened, so that they do not altogether injure nor are they altogether injured, as they used to injure and be injured before the creation of the world. And there will come a time when this power of injury which still subsists in them will be brought to an end through the doctrine which is coming to pass at the new mixture. And in the establishment of that new world, all the evil motions will cease and all rebellions will come to an end; the foolish will be persuaded and deficiencies will be filled up, and there will be peace and tranquillity by the gift of Him who is Lord of all Natures."

In this long abstract of the argument of the *De Fato* I have purposely given a very free translation, or rather paraphrase, because our object has been to follow the thought more than the actual language. It is difficult to realise how an ancient work of this kind appeals to other people; but to myself, coming from the study of ordinary Syriac ecclesiastical literature, the first impression made is of the independence of the writer's mind. It gives me the impression of being the thoughts of one who had learned to think for himself, one who had read much and thought much, and who was not content at the end merely to repeat the formulas of a school. Bardaisan brings out of the storehouse of his learning things new and old, and his imagination has woven them into a new and independent pattern. Such work is of a different order from that of men whose whole achievement is to reproduce as much of the philosophy of someone else — of Aristotle or of Proclus —as they have been able to understand.

The next reflexion of the student of ecclesiastical history will be that the Syriac-speaking Church was not able to retain Bardaisan in its communion. You have heard the argument of the *De Fato*, and you are in a position to appreciate the ideas which the School of Bardaisan cherished "on God, on Nature, and on human Life." That the *De Fato* really comes from the School of Bardaisan is certain, whether or no Bardaisan had a share in the actual literary composition of it; and I am quite sure that it gives a far truer picture of the spirit which animated Bardaisan and his disciples than the spiteful polemic of S. Ephraim or the unintelligently repeated catchwords which are echoed by various late chroniclers. But in that case we must feel it a pity that the Church made Bardaisan into a heretic. The whole Dialogue is pervaded by an admirable spirit. It is marked by reverence towards the Lord of all things and by gratitude for His benefits, by cheerful obedience to the ordinary discipline of the Church, by courtesy towards opponents, and above all by a firm faith that the Judge of all the earth will not do injustice. Less admirable perhaps from the narrower ecclesiastical standpoint is the firm and clear determination not to do violence to the facts of nature and of life. The writer refuses to shut his eyes to what he sees around him at the bidding of a theory, and his field of vision was not limited to Church History and the Old Testament. It was doubtless Bardaisan's independence of mind that led to his excommunication. We dare not press the details of the story of how Bishop 'Aqai "warned" him, but it is easy to imagine the scene. We may fancy the difficulties which Bardaisan's learned theories may have caused when caught up by ignorant brethren. We may fancy the bishop waiting on the philosopher, a man great both by birth and by achievement, and requesting him to modify his views. May we not go on to imagine that Bardaisan heard him out, listening at first with amused courtesy, and then when the Churchman proved deaf alike to explanation and to reasoning, accepting without much searching of heart the sentence of ostracism from the Christians' conventicle? This is mere fancy; but in sober fact it was a regrettable incident. We know next to nothing of the history of the School of Bardaisan, save that Rabbûla induced the remaining members to submit to the Church, some century and a quarter after. By that time the mischief had been done. We can see how grievously the Syriac-speaking Church suffered by failure to attract and to bear with the best scientific intellect of the time. It is a foolish and cowardly policy for a Church to be tolerant to superstition and rigid towards reverent speculation. The Syriac-speaking Church ultimately sank into formal heresies, while the great mass of the populations of the East adopted the new faith of Islam; I cannot help wondering how much of the collapse may have had its roots in intellectual cowardice.

Life and progress mean change, the rejection of what is worn-out or unsuitable as well as mere development; the mere "keeping one's wicket up," to adopt the phrase championed by the Bishop of Worcester, can only issue in stagnation. And the story of Bardaisan is being enacted over again just outside our own doors. It has been impossible to study Bardaisan's career without thinking of the case of the Abbé Loisy. The parallel is all the closer if there be anything in the tradition which puts Bardaisan into Holy Orders. Moreover, both writers are known for their treatises against heretics: Bardaisan wrote against Marcion and *l'Évangile et l'Église* is a defence of the Catholic Church against the Protestantism of Dr Harnack. But the inner resemblance is independent of these external circumstances. The essential point of resemblance is that M. Loisy, like Bardaisan, takes account of the Science which exists outside the narrow bounds of ecclesiastical study. He recognises its validity and its claim to judge those portions of ecclesiastical tradition which lie within its own sphere. To recognise this is to recognise that part of the traditional presentation of Christianity and part of its traditional defences must be modified from time to time if we are to retain the chief point, namely that our philosophy of religion shall be firmly based on observed facts and not erected on a flimsy scaffolding to correspond with some ideal plane, a scaffolding liable to collapse when the supports are removed or undermined. Bardaisan was declared a heretic, M. Loisy has been condemned by the Holy Office; may the intellectual paralysis which overspread the Syriac Churches be averted from our own Church and the Church of Rome!

There is one thing in conclusion upon which I should be glad to lay stress. The Dialogue *On Fate* is in form a dispute between a Christian and an unconverted heathen: the question of how the grace of God reaches the individual is not discussed, nor was any opinion dealing with this subject included among the heresies of Bardaisan. The main question actually in dispute between Bardaisan and Awida was whether such a thing as Free-will in man exists, and what was the sphere of its activity. It is a question still discussed, though I suppose the advocates of Free-will tend to become more diffident. What, then, is the argument upon which Bardaisan is not afraid to rely? Bardaisan's theory is that the sphere of Free-will is mainly restricted to the building up of the individual character, and his argument for the existence of this moral Free-will is that the Christian Faith produces in those who embrace it a corresponding change of character, a change that can be seen and known of all men. Can we, dare we, use that argument now? I do not propose to follow up the philosophical conclusions involved, if the facts be granted. I can only speak as a student of ancient history. What I wish to point out is that the victory which overcame the ancient world actually meant a change in the individual's life, and that it was the mark of a living faith to influence the conduct. Whatever may be the philosophical explanation, the member of the ancient Christian Church—Bardaisan the heretic, as much as Justin Martyr—really felt within him a new and constraining force. That force was not possessed, or not possessed to anything like the same extent, by the opponents and rivals of Christianity. Half the jealousy with which the official world regarded the Church was due to the consciousness that the source from which the Church drew its life and its force lay outside and independent of the State. What gave Christianity this force is another question, but the early Christians were well aware of it, and we shall never understand the history of the rise of Christianity unless we remember its existence. That inward force is the real, indispensable Note of the true Church: the future will belong to the Church only if she is able to supply the constraining power over individual conduct, to the evident effects of which Bardaisan was not afraid to appeal.

EDESSA.
View looking N.N.W.

[To face p. 193.

www.ingramcontent.com/pod-product-compliance
Lightning Source LLC
Chambersburg PA
CBHW031255230426
43670CB00005B/203